The American Poetry Review/Honickman First Book Prize

The Honickman Foundation is dedicated to the support of projects that promote spiritual growth and creativity, education and social change. At the heart of the mission of the Honickman Foundation is the belief that creativity enriches contemporary society because the arts are powerful tools for enlightenment, equity and empowerment, and must be encouraged to effect social change as well as personal growth. A current focus is on the particular power of photography and poetry to reflect and interpret reality, and, hence, to illuminate all that is true.

The annual American Poetry Review/Honickman First Book Prize offers publication of a book of poems, a $3,000 award, and distribution by Copper Canyon Press through Consortium. Each year a distinguished poet is chosen to judge the prize and write an introduction to the winning book. The purpose of the prize is to encourage excellence in poetry, and to provide a wide readership for a deserving first book of poems. *Evidences* is the sixth book in the series.

Winners of The American Poetry Review/Honickman First Book Prize

Joshua Beckman *Things Are Happening* 1998

Dana Levin *In the Surgical Theatre* 1999

Anne Marie Macari *Ivory Cradle* 2000

Ed Pavlić *Paraph of Bone & Other Kinds of Blue* 2001

Kathleen Ossip *The Search Engine* 2002

James McCorkle *Evidences* 2003

Evidences

Evidences

James McCorkle

Winner of The APR/Honickman First Book Prize

The American Poetry Review

Philadelphia

 Direct all inquiries to: The APR/Honickman First Book Prize, *The American Poetry Review*, 117 South 17th Street, Suite 910, Philadelphia, PA 19103.

Distribution by Copper Canyon Press/Consortium.

Library of Congress Catalogue Card Number: 2003090771

ISBN 0-9718981-3-8 (cloth, alk. paper)
ISBN 0-9718981-4-6 (pbk., alk. paper)
First edition

Designed by Adrianne Onderdonk Dudden
Composed by Duke & Company

Acknowledgments:
Boulevard: "Bee-Yards" and "Early Betrayals"
Colorado Review: "The Sand Runs Through [. . . *Es Rinnt Uns der Sand aus den Haaren*]" and "Numerology"
Conjunctions/web: "Canaan"
Fiddlehead: "The Lamprey" and "The Anchor"
Kenyon Review: "Reading Bashō to My Daughter" and "What is Wanted"
Mānoa: "Cryptography" and "Pyromancy"
New England Review: "Infidelities"
Ploughshares: "Iron Path [*Eisen-Steig*]"
I am grateful to the National Endowment for the Arts for a fellowship during which some of these poems were written.
I wish to thank Jorie Graham for her support and Elizabeth Scanlon for her care. The friendship and advice over the years of Phillis Levin, Mary Caponegro, and Michael Ives have been incalculable.

for Cynthia, Katharine and Ara

Contents

Introduction

"It would be here," this extraordinary first book begins. *Here,* the place and the condition which requires of us, firstmost, presence. Which precedes, by definition, for this poet—as for his Romantic and Modernist predecessors—any *now.* Aptly enough, this *here,* the Dickinsonian *here* of a soul "wrecked, solitary, here"—is first announced in a poem—one of a number—titled "Estuarine." For the sensation of that so-exact yet blurry spot where river enters sea, as it is itself entered by sea, seems the very spot the soul, in this book, on its x/y coordinates of here and now, crucified on the natural world, seeking resurrection, inhabits to find bearings.

And bearings it finds: firstmost sensorial, in the fullness of the body's loss, its seizure of and full embrace of, time; then in the fullness of the mind's embrace of what the body gives it, incarnate, to know: "pressured by its fullness"; and then by the precise apprenticeship to knowledge afforded by the senses those poets who trust the body find: Bashō, Wordsworth, Dickinson, Hopkins—both of the poems and of the journals—Williams, Ammons, Niedecker, Charles Wright. "It would be here what is as / Abstract as light finds its measure, / Heaping up in weight, the sky / Pressured by its fullness, where everything / Is below surface, below light's press."

That the poem moves from phenomenological perception to the literal world of ray and eel-grass, of swarm, transparent spawn, silt and mudflows, toxins, slow spillage, dampnesses, seepages, in the very next lines, is typical of its spirit-knowledge of how mysteriously, organically and effortlessly, the abstract courses down the tiniest slope of thought to pick up, carry, and be carried by, its material grains. "A geometry of understanding" this poet calls his work, and, indeed, *Evidences* keeps exploring the question, the crucial spiritual question of to what extent hope—or new life—rises from the far side (intimation, inspiration), rather from the near side (human will). Perhaps that is why McCorkle turns so insistently, and instinctively, to the very smallest lifematter in his everpresent garden—"spiking of bracken and mullein," for example . . . Yes, there may be menace (as one hears in the word "spiking"), but the feature of these small emergences resembles a script which this poet feels it is his vocation to decipher and to literally, as if alchemically, summon into presence.

That this imagination can move, even more extraordinarily, from its deep apprenticeship to the biological (and geographic and geologic) to the outmost reaches of not only history, but historical atrocity, in poems that track and engage Anselm Kiefer's paintings, is one of the great wonders of the book. That it manages to find a verbal equivalent for both Kiefer's and Celan's alchemical use of the matter of their medium—difficult in the extreme in the case of words—is an even greater wonder. "Broken forms," he calls them early on, but they are only fractured and "shifting always towards description, as if that were the beginning / for truth" . . . for "to describe is to slow / The sifting of losses."

So it is that the surface of things is, therefore, a variously permeable membrane, part deposit, part deposition, "where to know implies re-entry." His language itself becoming often thickly textured because working through the question of transparency or permeability. Is the page itself—is language—permeable, impermeable?

This confrontation with loss—in the guise of loss of vision—is patient, relentless, sometimes even cheered by the sheer multitude of things there are to *be* lost, by how powerful the adversary *is.* In fact, one feels the imagination push up and take the measure of the adversary—loss and destruction of the human and inhuman kind—and become amplified rather than reduced, linguistically, by the size of the task. There are more kinds of poems here than I normally see in one book—more philosophical speculation, narrative, meditation, passionate description, lyrical eddying, monologuist asides, front-facing addresses; and more ways of "facing," in fact, than one could imagine finding under the tonal range of one voice, and such a powerfully consistent one at that. All of which make the urgency of the poetic activity, its brutal honesty—as well as its lush commitment to the fullness of the record of undoings—simultaneously terrifying and vivifying. One wants to live in a world so very brimful of what one loves and yet so equally full of its destruction: I do not believe it is possible to miss how brave this book is, how daring, and given over to beauty—both in its surface and in its love of what is on our surfaces—and yet, how unwilling it is, still, ever, to avert its gaze from the images that are slowly immolating that which remains in excess of one's knowledge.

McCorkle's interest in Kiefer is related to this severe adhering perception of, and acute attention to, that immolation and excess. Beginning with its acute attention to the four elements, and to the alchemical properties of the world, all in *Evidences* attaches to his passionate belief in the transmutation of the base into the refined. Consequently, as he has to do the work of refinement in a world where the materials are especially resistent, we can watch him, in so many poems, grow most interested in where things go in and out of vision—partly because, in truth, any access to "things" is obviously seriously compromised. What makes him stay committed, and us so deeply, emotionally engaged, is the degree to which his interfacings with reality are urgent in tone, and comprised of so many different strategic actions: the limits of focus, the limits of form, the saturation of history, the degradation of language. So that the poems ask us to focus on many forms of seepage, on spawning places, on oozings, beginnings, sources of all kinds—origins —promisings—but always where there is danger, always where there are toxins. One could say McCorkle's essential vision, his drama, takes place in the narrow zone between toxin and spawn. And yet the poems, formally as well as experientially, are beautifully aerated as well. This is a poet who, for all his commitment to the thicknesses of texture, is equally attuned to breath, to freshness, to tracings and overtracings. Of course—and here again his signature dilemma—the more the transparent tracings overlap, making for truth, the less visible the real becomes; the more fully responsible he becomes, the more illegible the surface becomes. And yet all this drama exists in tension with an extraordinary desire for transparency—which we witness, foremost, in the sublime clarity of his style, and accuracy of his description.

For survival seems to attach, in the end, to a straightforward view, to a story that can be told, a story worth telling, by the poet to his young daughter, a story about spring, a story to help us—as so many of these poems seek to do—make it through winter—winter oncoming, winter settled indefinitely upon us. Everywhere, in this stunning work, the poet seeks out equivalents for the springs of emotion, inklings of consciousness, the dream of water in drought that awakens one to actual water—a water made of syllables and breath—"as though to suck the beginning back, / To find its taste again," because

> Then is artesian, rock cleft, what begins, or means to be,
> And now,
>
> What is there, opening out, calyx, hyacinth, water meadow,
> The O's of fish tasting the other element . . .

Jorie Graham

1

Estuarine

It would be here, the light soaring
Above the grasses, the flats that stretch

Across a bay or river gap, here the light
Molten, the birds glints

Of turned glass, the wash of things
In and out of vision, the water pushing

Out flat, tarnished, tannin seeped,
It would be here what is as

Abstract as light finds its measure,
Heaping up in weight, the sky

Pressured by its fullness, where everything
Is below surface, below light's press.

The movement of ray and eel-grass
In the outflow, the swarm of transparent

Spawn, ciphers of the next season.
In the silt and mudflows

Toxins graphed, slow spillage
As across an icon, dampness, seepage from

Gutters, a blistering wall, the blue
Green turning powdery,

Distances obscured, such sacred
Vistas lost now, the birds white

On white, the light pouring down,
What we know hurts us, and
What isn't known waits,

Its necessity a geometry of understanding
Each angle's addition.

And light swarms,
The stretch of water could be

Apprehended only as light, the world
As light alone, speechless here

Except that, that single expanse,
Something nothing can penetrate, they said.

The Sand Runs Through
[. . . *Es Rinnt Uns der Sand aus den Haaren*]

The script runs across the top, lined, it must be
Recollections, someone lost in the wastes of silica and hematite

Below, as though looking into a valley, clusters
Of rectangles, as though mud bricks had loosened, a collapsed wall,

Cordage, brown tangle over the pubis, over sand, over
Recollections, and further, the chaos of broken forms, the sand

Sifting between them in the wind, minute dry rivers,
Shifting always toward description, as if that were the beginning

For truth, be it told, or its recollection, to describe is to slow
The sifting of losses, the always ready trope as the script

Dries across the top, the cracking surface releases the last
Moisture to the air, but that was long ago, as the writer

Would have noted had the lines run on, and her hand not
Tired, the embargo set in place, the plains blasted with salt

---

The age, your age and mine. A deposition.
Fixed and documented. The appearance
Of lines, denotations, silver splatters on the photographs,
Lines creasing surfaces. Here is my desert,
Skin over my heart, pulled taut across the fan
Of my hand. Our windows opened out across
That expanse, the air brittle with sand.
In the mountains, families chisel
Fossils from the marl of ancient seabeds,
How long would it take a bird to traverse that expanse,

To find harbor, you ask. Here is the photograph
Of where this age set forth, the air filled with sand
And salt blown from the sea leagues away. The sky's skin
Peeling. In the desert everything is mirage,
Liquid, blue mercury, a prayer traced in the sand
Makes its own maze before swept away
Without our escaping. The messages pile up,
Meanwhile sand washes over the roads.
In our time, this was not to have happened,
That catalogue of disasters and depletions,
Some never forecast, but arriving all the same.
Sometimes steady, a drought. Others, sudden,
Dwellings leveled, shorn olive trees, rutted tracks.

And then,
There is the drifting, incessant accumulations
That render featureless the place,

An altered state, boundaries moved
Through daily crossfire and stonings
To briefly mark this

As the site of which atrocity, or that moment
You opened which window, the sea there
Incandescent with phosphor

Secreted from swarms of fish and algae,
Swirling in their own scripts, or meanwhile
There the impossibility of leaving

This scene always in drag, arriving again
And again, strapped with munitions
Or slung with animal pelts and butchered meat,

Coming out of the forest, at the edge of the clearing,
Then at your door bearing a suitcase of vials,
You opened your window to owls

Flying from pines, the sea a maze of color,
Remembering, then, walking in the desert
You whispered the stars too

Must be homeless, the desert the place of
His absence, that which was the gift
Or that which was taken away,

You whispered, in the sand the marks of bodies
Stretch out among twisted wood,
As examples, lost, as warnings, figures of evidence

The Hibernaculum

A late frost browned the early peonies.
The world is always starting.
The fear of it makes myth—the chambers
Daubed with it until they shone.

And the world divided into ours and theirs.
What could be said, and not.
What was shaped from the forms of doubt.
What came out of sleep and approached, or not.

Afterward, a flow of snakes, bursting
As though an artesian spring
Had cracked open the ground. Uncoiling,
Sleep draining from hearts.

Through the hillside's spiking bracken and mullein,
Dispersing and at each conjunction what was
Before, now only implied, to know implies re-
Entry, the abode, the overwintering bee.

And again, driven in by the blood-slowing cold, prey
And devourer together in a capsule of sleep,
A dark chambered garden before dispersal
Through orchards and fields.

To wing-sheen and eye-prism, snake-belly—
If we could lift them from their nest of sleep,
A medusa's coil—our scorn fills
Their pits, catches on the stiff fur of thoraxes.

Then fall under talons' shadows, spring the remarriage
Of devoured and devouring, where all
Has been sent out to dig or hunt—
The shrew or wood-mouse, osprey or corn-snake, willow or ash.

Where offspring eat the father, the father devours the sons
And beds the daughters without sorrow,
For where would we be with sorrow
Or the absolution of violence?

And what of volition, to rouse out of the sleep,
The earth warm, for a moment pastoral,
A memory made from bleached straw
And cracking varnish.

But scented with urine and sleep's ejaculations,
Stinking—we hate the smell of animal,

But when you or I dreamed of being
Adonis or Aphrodite we washed ourselves with animal fat.

And rendered, what—consolation for being
Driven out, or mercy fashioned
By stake or camp, or solace in
That it was him and not you.

Birth of the Sun [*Geburt der Sonne*]

All day rain seemed woven into air, imminent

Along the coastal highway, the fog narrowed, orchards, reefs below

That night, the wolves were swimming beneath our windows, I saw them when I woke

The syllables, recounting that time, congest

Then there was that night, the film caught it all

The huge bombers spiraled out of the sky, afire, all night falling

The particularities condense of their own accord

And in the late works, registering the erosion of older linguistic structures

Bombers falling, alight, splintering into the grass

I recall the fur, wet, ragged, as they plunged in the dark water flecked with weed

In the strict measure of time, their falling took

It could have been forever, undisclosed, lost, bursting over, the air ringing

Conduit, portal, the new grammar of cumulation

I was holding you while they passed

After they passed, the night's fricatives rose in pitch

The figures resumed their mounting

Distress calls across the lagoon

It would have been a brief silvering of the sky

They dropped like solder, mercury falling

Whether I open the window or not, they will be there, or coming back

Always more, the levels of saturation compound to an altered state

A system bearing more than conditions allow

What are the ways of addressing the pilot wrapped in solder and falling

That condition built on measurable quantities moving through fixed conduits

Your pulse as I held you

Every passage marks a retreat, an elision of subject

Whereas the wolves, moving—there, there, there

• • •

What does it mean to lend consistency to the presence of someone *when the very images we examine are slowly immolating* *Or to assume* an event has occurred along with an immanent break taking the sustained form of a faithful process *What can perseverence refer to and in its continuity can one be faithful to what one does not know* *That part of one which one does not know or has access to or that remains beyond or in excess of one's knowledge*

• • •

Watching the footage of air strikes over Hanoi filmed and narrated by those on the ground

• • •

It was not long after that

• • •

What we were looking for, written, Evil is the process of a simulacrum of truth
And in its essence, under a name of its invention, it is terror directed at everyone
But in this always comes betrayal   How were we seized by it   To make it ours
Or if not it ours, to turn its presence into our own invention, new systems of delivery, disclosures, deportations, detentions, the mechanics for the continuity of this invention

• • •

If it is always preceded by good, then we are trapped in a system of origins

• • •

The dream was recorded: a walled city, the angels along the parapets, the palms and gardens glimpsed toward the center of the complex, itself, in retrospect a maze, but the dreamer able to scale the walls and glimpse toward the interior, before an angel's sword, all fire, cast the dreamer out (again) onto the sands, the dreamer knowing this was neither dream nor event, but upon waking could only be categorized within a system of oppositions

• • •

We are now not unlike them, watching the plane streak overhead, dropping in altitude, a shadow overtaking us

• • •

That rip in one,
The heavy atom hammered apart,
Birth of sun, and rod, and rain; then
In the dust and glass and lead
A coat, ashen dresses, little is left
Of time, O darling Ones

The Burning of the Rural Districts
[*Ausbrennen des Landkreises Buchen*]

the difficult way
the book charred
shadows across
in the book put into
question the
original and copy

the path
and what we are on
to where
as smoke rises past that copse

thus the word
painting   tree   corpse
there and there and there
which was left out
the heaps of them

that way each morning
successive hills scrim

was it
those who walked this way gone
though the record will show
or imply we have washed our hands of it

as though it could be
be but an object
left eccentric   otherwise
or outside
any knowing
the rural districts were burned

assembling the found
questions authenticity in so far as
which and why that one or
on the furrows' octaves jabbed crows
or as in somewhere we began this

at that edge the passage started
crows in air
like smoke you say
and always the suspicion

of beginnings
what put you on this track you ask

no wild iris
here
nothing to draw you or hold you here

heaps   furrows
Oh copse, where we sang, once
something always returns   a bit of song
a tooth   a broken jar   all
birds on wing   like smoke you say again

again   as though I was not listening
all I had was a picture charred
ashes set between the pages of the book
which town was that   its name   its name

like bell   or wood   or birch always burning

Infidelities

Wet air, rain oncoming,
And carrying with it brine
And creosote, harbor and breakwater,
Scent of spray and shipwreck,
Not inland rain. This is air
Hollowed to bear the traces
Of other geographies across the landscape.
With such randomness this scent
Arrives, almost like the discovery
Of an infidelity, unknown until
It surrounds us, the wind blowing
The backs of leaves, silvering
Like fresh spawn when something
Rises suddenly from below them.

The scent of wet air is brief,
Turning dark and thin,
Betraying itself, until it becomes
Memory, unhealed, repeating
Like forsythias, each late April
Blooming across the hillside,
Before sicklewort, larkspur, or yarrow
Begin to cure the air, draw
The wounds dry. Time heals, some
Console. Shafts of hollyhocks
Bloom by deep summer: infusions
Could be made to calm memory
Or dye anger, but past the trees
Lie ruined harbors the air still pulls from.

The world resumes. For one, infidelity
Reveals desire never rests with only one,
And for another, infidelity is
Deportation, a rusted ship waits:
Again, we are meant to learn to suffer
At another's pleasure, and to enter the world again
As it is, itself betrayed already by those before us.
The hillsides begin their own work of summer:
Myrtle's blue covers the ground, the scent of allium drifting . . .
For the one who is faithless, there is nothing
To add, the world resumes with its
Consequences already discounted.
And for the others, their words have been
Pulled from their dark hold, and cast down.

The New Season

Trees well into green pyres,
The path full of petals,
                    everything in flood.
Drenched by lilacs
               gathered after a late night walk,
Alphabets of fragrances spin

Across the lake
              after a wind storm,
Carrying their messages for this one life.
Everything is a guide,
                   I had thought,
But then the world would be here
Only to keep us from becoming lost—

Birds rise
         in fevered astonishment,
The sky stained by lupines—
                     the world is here,
And going without need of ourselves.

The tips of trees point to the sky.
Between tar-streaked
                 buildings ocher-green showers
Of willows curtain the lake.

Gulls rise—white-caps—
                      then slide out of view
With the idea of the soul,
                     the years have filtered
To thin sediments, the air a puzzle of flies and pollen.

No words outside this landscape's domain—
Nothing is periphery,
            disappearing, sabotaged, refused—
Only this world, this accord.

The Instance of Water

Some water travels underground, in rivers that flow for miles
Sometimes only a few feet underground
Then re-surface as a series of ponds,
Or a stretch of stream that disappears in a marsh or lake.

Flowing through limestone, water hollows, the ground above
Collapses, the caverns creating new lakes.
Dye has been released in some to determine
The extent of passageways:

Red swirls vanish, then with schools of bream
And goatfish, surface miles later in another lake:
Divers try to follow, every summer, those threads;
Reports of someone lost, the silt stirred,

The cave narrowing until there is no room
To turn, air-tanks empty and narcosis settles.
Schools of fish splinter into light in the clear water.
Walking across such a terrain,

The ground turns soft, brush turns to marsh weeds—
A blister, where water forms a bubble
And osmotically seeps into light:
Is this how it all began, someone walking,

Then disappearing into the ground, swept
Into an unknown river, carried off
As though on a white bull's back to sea, garlands
Of flowers left in the wake, washed ashore.

Or in another place, at a ledge, over a lake
That divers say has no bottom, but find volcanic shelving

Where gold cups and headbands rest
In the silt, hearts then bodies were thrown

And must have drifted weighted endlessly downwards:
Leaving the city in retreat.
The horsemen and armored footmen
Were so weighted with gold

They floundered in rivers and canals radiating
From the city, and drowned—swept, too,
Away, with the sacrificed whose souls
By then were the swarms of hummingbirds

Above Tenochtitlán, as their hearts must still be
Drifting toward a molten center.
While walking, if water is flowing close
Underground, why haven't I heard it,

Or will I only when it is too late, the sound coming
As if from a distant waterfall,
Even as I am pulled in, swallowed alive,
As though by shark, serpent, or crocodile—

This is how it could have started,
A story about one disappearing into the mouth
Of the earth or sea or sky—and hearing the shouts,
Some might turn and watch, only later

Thinking that I might have been pulled
Free, but stood and watched, as though
To prepare for the beginning of guilt,
The denial that such things could happen,

To place the blame elsewhere, the invention of gods.
Or is the whisper of water underground
That of the gods, their only warning, heard
Like a breath at night on my neck, while a hawk circled

With no prey in sight, the land below
Stretching dry and soulless below it.
The instance of water, beading up,
A garland of lakes, beyond the curve of its eye.

This would be the world waiting,
The dry caves without drawings, empty salt-pans,
The rain knotted in the sky, invisible, for a moment
At the beginning everything absolutely still.

Disruptive Patterning

Think of it this way as
Verticals moving against verticals,
Derivations from the local,

Think of it as derivative but
Changing, moving in the high grass,
One body, think of it

As the life of the spirit, once
And for all, exposed but still
Moving in the high grass,

Hidden from itself, moving
Against its own appearance.
Think of it this way

Then, as it shifts, that
Way before the sun's caldron,
Shadows stepped into and then out,

Its body, out of touch from ourselves,
The high grasses brushing
The body itself a place among

Places, its spirit not culled
From itself, think of it then
As it moves, spirit and all,

Through the high grasses,
A stranger we make from its
Plural form into the singular

Determining, think of it as
Not an unfolding, a name
Floated across the space

We thought was shared, but
Separate, think of the world itself as
God moving through the stiffened

Grass, each blade creased,
The body passing through the high
Grass exposed but already secret.

A dialogue between parts, the sky
                    bearing down its persistent
Thickening of gray,

The deterioration of conditions,
A thaw ends, out along the paths
                    looking for new shoots

I am too early, tracks cross
                    the path, no sign of stopping,
The winter sun a burnished place in the cloud-cover,

"Wrap yourself up. Vanish," is the advice,
Moving in declension,
                    to ravine or frozen lake bed,

Snow blown from trees, gobbets
Of light descending through their forms,

The future in dispersal, deposed,
Where nothing shines and steps forward

Out of cross-hatch and interval.

Memory, too, is like that—
Expiation for something left undone and always
The rumor of what was found

Splendid by friends in Tangier,
Years ago, or earlier, sunburned at a picnic table
The water over your shoulder, past the dunes,

Almost green at noon. Now, calling it all
Back in, the shuffle of photographs,
And who's been dealt in, again,

Who's been left spinning, silken, wrapped
For the long empty haul,
Past the children's voices at yard's end.

What is left to believe—it all starts again,
That's the trick we play on ourselves
Rubbing our hands on the nubbed

Hawthorn branches, breaking one,
Its green heart laid open—
If, then, we could unravel a message,

It would send us out alone,
Branch against sky,
Shadow against ground, the old press

Of contraries, the law of here and gone,
Bearing us away, across
The sodden mat of grass in a February thaw.

Star-Gown [*Sterntaler*]

In the almost ever present
cornflowers clasped w/ olive leaves
& wrapped around
a core of papyrus pith, the colors almost
present, or acacia garlands
w/ lotus & poppy petals
colors lingering after their airless sojourn,
those final offerings, laid by the last departing
ones, preparations for that after-
life completed, the river running through it, too,
ocher and lifeless,
heron and hawk in the reeds.
Or fig leaves left,
but entering the chamber
turned to dust once touched, did the traveler
reach home, such leavings
for us only, our reminders of that
ephemeral moment—a door opened,
hawk setting wing—river moving
w/ its pestilence, carrying persea leaves north,
what remains these are, verging
on dust, the stars moving through
their passages, clear, direct
in the chamber overhead.
& what rises from
that shroud wrapped around,
that was what was left, there
the last petals scatter'd when
the door opened

Leopardi wrote, translating, illusions "are essential ingredients in the system of human nature, and given by nature to each and every man, in such a way that it is not right to scorn them as the dreams of one alone, but really and truly of man and desired by nature, and without which our life would be the most miserable and barbarous thing." Reading this in the dust and lead, the sky in a swirl of vapor, the syntaxes assembling in their contagion wards, O, the world, the world, the resistance to its barbarity, the acids in the film strips and plates of images graven and silvering into one lasting sheen.

---

that, wrapped around,
letting the ocher
cloud exhale from
its wrappings,
night-shift,
star spores
exposed
on the glass plates
the field turns bright
a single element, radiative
and the idea of
afterwards, when everything
is onrushing outward
so that
the event is there
and there, its horizon
between, a thin line
moving, curling into
planar form and
back, the there and there

turning, a field under fire
field of fire, field of lightning, stars
in their fields, wrapping
their dust about us, we
that watch that

The gap was there: we were listening for what could find no sound, no whisper, or utterance. If what was to be addressed could not be addressed, how could we proceed, how could what we did hear align with what could not be heard, what had not even a whisper. And then those bits left behind, the smoke trailed sentences, pretexts for what could not be heard. And this is the shift, that whisper of letters is beyond hearing, for who was there beside you, and in that condition, whose words are yours but yours, whispering down to me, listening, but beyond hearing.

The clouds coalesced, lit by moon, what solitary one
Is there, at the shore, the wind carrying the sand
And spray, the night wrapping about the figure,
Thick air, marine and black, the moon there, but just
The disk of light that has no passage outward, the tips
Of clouds retreat into their lightless domains, first
And last figure, you, what can be claimed for you,
Coming as you do, solitary at the margin—and ourselves,
Claiming you our lost daughter, lost in the dust
Our lost father, lost in fire, our lost twin lost speaking
To us; in all the places of perishing, you are
There, stained and under the moon that is no more
Than a disk, first and last, at last no one we know
But ourselves—emptied of desire, of final requests—passing.

11

Cryptography

Between May's Pond and the Main Pool
Marsh grass, cat-tails bow
                    slantwise blown—

Maples hung in yellow,
Veined in cinnabar anthocyanins.

Geese have begun to land,
Knowing the signature of this place
By its pull from the north

As the light breaks apart
On the thin waters of the ponds.

In the clear-cut, the land driven to pasture
Between Junius Ponds, there is less
Memory of what was before
                    heaps of stones

With old mosses—
Marginalia for what was here.

Chain-link and barbed-wire,
The air fills with ice-thorns
That catch on my clothes,
Whole constellations scatter from the reeds.

What holds in this life—
                hawk on a post
At the marsh edge, waiting for mouse or hare
While I-90 carries its wind and ash west,
The smell of gasoline cuts

The marsh in half—
                    at the height of summer

The sky an apse of blue,
A Sunday afternoon, on a track
Along Esker Brook,
After the trillium and jack-in-the-pulpits
Had died back
And the flies had risen into their one song
That could persist forever,
A group of Amish, six men and six women,
Passed me in the splotched sunlight,
Walking toward the deeper woods.

A spider's web pulled taut across the path—
They have gone another way,
While I duck around it,
Ready to head back home, leaving it air-hung,
Its study uninterrupted.

The brook almost dry,
Maybe it runs only with snow-melt
Or a wet summer—
                    blue-tipped
Black dragonflies cling to the leaf-edge
Of dock or plantain—
                    in us all
No word is lost, however the leaves
Tilt upwards, dry.

Rising late each night since summer
My heart rides up, close to my skin
As though I were in thin air,

Looking across the locked yards
And tight houses,
I think my soul has left me—
                        as if this were proof
Then of having a soul,
Its departure—

                The wind stirs the vines
Outside the window—
                  under the moon, the sandbars
Must glow in the marsh,
Like figures
In script, herons in slate waters
        redwings on the whip of a reed
            martins driven into the lightening sky.

Pyromancy

Poised above salvia and impatiens,
The pair arrived like green tears—

I had not seen any since moving from the other side
Of the continent until this summer—
                                                  arriving on spun arcs,

As if traced by a steady hand, lines like hot glass
Pulled across the garden's profusion.

They follow a tide of flower-blooming north to here,
That at August breaks and retreats

Toward the Gulf of Mexico, the Yucatán, the Caribbean,
Toward the sun.

Afraid to move, we watch,
Knowing they are messengers flying from the cups
Of bromeliads and the flesh of orchids,

Their feathers igniting with light
In the trees' high canopies.

Along the Pacific, they would swarm in certain trees,
Trumpet flowers and flame vines,
                                              clacking at each other,
Sun-forged and hovering.

Then one by one they soared into the white sky of afternoon,
To watch their flight hurt our eyes
As though we had stitched our sight to invisibility

As they drew distance to the point of an acetylene flame;
Each heart tightened its valves—
                                        the sky opening its blue door to them.

In Mexico, among the Zinacantán, they were likened to bats,
Both nectar-seekers and aerialists,
One the summer, the other winter;

The bat, jaguar, raven, woven into one emblem,
The weak sun of December;
The hummingbird a hawk or eagle, the sun itself,

Their migrations must have been seen
As nothing less than the departure of souls southward,
Carried on their jeweled mantles,
In their eyes summer storms rising from the gulf.

Incarnations, messengers, incarnations,
The density of the species drops
Exponentially further from the tropics, until here there is only one,
Ruby-throated male, both green as the inner aura of a flame.

We go outside ourselves to watch—
As small as the morning star floating on the sky,

Its flight, unrehearsed, tests what is here
And not here, what has been released
And what remains hidden—

The color of unopened flowers, scent.
The flowers listen for their arrival.

In one thing another becomes and then passes on
To the next, resplendent to dark and back,
And yet there all the while—

A blue light that flashed off the Pacific or Gulf of Campeche,
Another sudden divinity that comes, evanescent,

Coming each summer, when the salvia turn to sparks
Among blades of freesia
And spiked globes of beebalm,

That stays with us through the winter, iridescing
The snow, the wings of crows,
The water running off our skin as we rise from the steaming bath.

The Lamprey

Then I thought of them
Swarming,
off the page, from their picture,
Mouths open, in turbid
Waters, nothing like them

I had found,
not the gar, or shovel-nosed shark, nor rockfish
Washed up, fly-crawled,

In the ebb-tide's mud.
But
There,
Swimming up, as though to greet,
tubes of flesh, gelatinous, boneless
no gills, a line of seven breathing holes
eel-smooth, sperm-whips

Swimming up-stream, up-lake into the bright world
The water-surface like trout, rainbow, silver, swimming to it
open-mouthed
while I floated downwards, into deeper water,

The light falling back,
its thin curtains rising,
Below, shapes drift,
bodies that have fallen earlier
Into the gulf: this is the way
Childhood ends—
what words
I was trying to say as water filled my lungs,
My mouth hanging open,

Turned into eddies, riptides pulled me farther
Out—like their spawn

From streams' folds of mud, and drift
With their anchor of sand or gravel,
Dredging the water with sieve-mouths—
And in this drifting
                                        clasp me, against the night—is this what we want

To say, as the bright world disappears, the bed soaked with sweat,
A child's fever peaking—

        stepping out of the ocean, fish hang from him, their jaws clamped, tongues drilling

                                                —Faces hovered down-turned,
The light flicked on, something pulls back,
Leaving me with my name called

As though it's only words from there on out,
                                                                names streaming like ribbons,
                                                    suctioned to what is now invisible—
                                            and memory begun.

The Anchor

An anatomy of anger could be
Filaments pulled tight as a snagged
Fishing line, something discarded and sunk

In the silty bottom;
                              an anchor we had lost
One summer, thinking we could find it,

Believing the bottom was pure sand, that we had
Memorized the shore's features, triangulated
The place the forty pound bell-anchor slipped its line

And set us adrift looking for trout or redfish,
Flounder or sheepshead, anything
On a bright, cutting winter afternoon.

The anchor line trailing, a white squiggle that should be taut
Against current and wind—onshore a hundred yards away

Pines bristle—
                        we always thought this the best weather
For trout,
                the bay cold and withdrawn, send the fish
Closer.
            A roofer I know tells me how he would never
Hit his daughter: he showed me his hand, heavy
And gouged, he would knock her flat he said

If he did and wanted to know what I believed—then warned me
About kids growing up. He must have done it once,

Open-palmed, to know this, and saw his child stagger back—but
This is only a guess. I don't really know.
He tells me his wife disciplines their children—he's here
as a warning against
Himself, a crow at the roof's crown in August.
We tell stories because we want
To be, I think, because there is another set of stories
Paying themselves out. All summer I waited

For him to finish his job, to drill holes in the underside, the soffits,
So the roof would breathe, but he never showed.
Nothing caught,
And pulling up the anchor line, limp and weightless—
Alone at the bow, I stared stupid at the water, my father

Behind me said nothing, letting me take this
Myself, following the line where it should go

Into the water, down, to loop the hank again, bowline knotted
Sure as though I was knotted to it, safe, for it must hold,
Now for twenty-five years,
a slow burn, a lesson about knots and
New anchors: I still think of that spot offshore, midway between
The Liar's Club pier
And a dead-end that spilled on to the beach.

The anchor is there,
aluminum gray, a soundless bell,
no corrosion that hollows
Out, only lime rosettes of barnacles fuse
And hold shape.
There are some who believe this life is meant only
For expiation, most of the rest of us live it

That way without knowing,
sometimes coming to a stupid man
Who once threw out an untied anchor, standing with his child
To tell them, man and child, a story
That hides everything, or tries to, because in this town
Everything gets around—a poison we all drink from.

Reading Bashō to My Daughter

1.

There are characters she says
She'll remember forever: the one for horse, for world,
The one for fire that looks as if it bursts
Into flame.
            But she'd rather read about frogs,
Things still in this world.

2.

What promises are held—
                    no road is the same,
Leaves rush across, ice blackens.
                              Where we go becomes
Less known as we approach.

The critics retort, "so what's new"—
But I can't think of any argument they have offered
That settles or reassures
The claim things of this world
                                        disappear—
                                                    the day bends at the horizon, stars
Shift out of the constellations, their stories
Breaking into pixels to recombine
Into other figures whose stories haven't arrived

But are already spinning toward us, their light arcing
From distant prominences, past each heliopause, the old arrangements
Still flooding past, waiting to be seen—nothing

Disappears, everything ends,
caught in passage,
Filaments of fire weave into, woven from mountain, horse, world.

3.

In the night a frog leaps, Bashō says, translated,
Into the pond's deep resonance,
Best known of his poems notes the commentator—
Everything becomes commentary,
Margins crowded, yet what we look for isn't there:

> the hills were not very far from the highroad, and scattered
> with numerous pools. It was the season of a certain species
> of iris called *katsumi*. So I went to look for it. I went from
> pool to pool, asking every soul I met on the way where I could
> possibly find it, but strangely enough, no one had ever heard
> of it, and the sun went down before I caught even a glimpse of it.

The iris waits,
indifferent to us, waiting for
The buds to unfurl, the sun heating the ponds insects glance off
Of—we need to be reminded of
This, so little time,
if we have to be
Governed so—what is the time of iris, of the frog's leap,
The pond, crusting at its edges by the height of summer?

4.

Then the screen will go blank, before
A word is entered,

Contact lost. The aspect of metaphors
That provides them with energy is that they keep

Filling the screen—ponds dot with duckweed,
The water black with silt in suspension, clouds,

A heron's shadow.
                    In mid-winter, I saw one crossing
The ice-locked marsh crossed-hatched in brown

Teezle and cat-tails, the sky pitted with starlings
Surging up from a sumac thicket then low across
A cornfield left unplowed. The heron, single,
A word coming always into the world,

Blue as slate,
                as mid-winter
When the world traveled into has wrapped itself
Inside its old skins, cold mud, leaf-mats.

5.

The world never dormant when you think about it—rhizomes
Spinning leaf-blades in their starchy flesh,
Pond-bottoms in gestation, the mold-black water sluggish, almost ice.

The wasp at work at the window, out of season,
Tracks across the field's mud and gritty snow-melt,
Scabs of buds on the hawthorn—its fruit black and scattered on the ground—

Certain constants with their own variables, what's known
Always coming undone: the pond's circumference has no measure,
Its depth no plumb-line—
                                        not a representation of uncertainty,

But our own movement, stitched between the leap and the sudden
Splash, between memory and knowing—
                                                                      if knowing is really only an odds-on gamble

Of recurrence. Winter light curves along the branches. We're rolling
The dice, coming up short.

6.

Constellations rise through bare trees,
What we wrote
                        a soft cloth over
The face of things,

Horse
        mountain
                        world
                                fire

Filaments of each character a stroke of memory
Assembling again and again on the screen
Your figures—

Horse   Mountain

World   Fire

Everything holds its own beginnings,
Nothing ever leaves—
The constellations tracking back,
The pond still
                    resonant when Bashō left, freshets of iris
Running up the mountain side no one visits,
                                                            in bloom, blue, yellow-ribbed throat,
The same we have, waiting,
Its rhizomes thickening, pearl buds of leaf-whorls, on the hillside

Where in summer
                            lights flick
On and off, holding us in that stillness between.

Canaan

1. Sortilege

The news is always of rapture

A plume of dust, the raking of ashes

What we mean provokes a shift in attention

The boundary becomes diffuse and continuous

Have you beheld the lights

It is always the brother will eat the limbs of his brother, the dog the dog, the lamb will look up with bloody muzzle, flies congressing

We are approaching a history where no one will remember

A world without AIDS

What we mean by poetry is not language simply marked nor socially categorized as marked

As the great dunes of the Sahara continued to encroach southward

The dog the dog, the ashes the ashes

What is significant is the approach to the condition, the duration where forgetting is conscious, before the condition already given is assumed always the given

Through repetition language becomes marked, departs from conventional social constructions

External travel was restricted

The dust the dust

What is significant is the southward encroachment, water sources turning saline, the thinning of vegetation, a blossoming tree we had never seen before

Pinned on its thorns birds, plumage blackened, eyes pitted

The news was of rapture, lights seen, plumes

Brother cast out by brother, to let the desert greet him

The condition has stabilized to that of a persisting epidemic

Death benefits to the bereaved have been eliminated

Reports revealed he was still conscious when dragged

Reports revealed the pit contained at least three-hundred

Reports revealed guidelines instructing the use of increased physical pressure

This included *shabeh, gambaz,* and *tiltul*

We are approaching a history

The lights the lights the lights were

Falling

2. An Autobiography

Geography is the primer for autobiography,
The mapping of a vicinity, what is
Kept in and cast out.

Who comes to the temple and who is barred,
The olive trees planted,
And those uprooted, cast in the desert.

Memory stricken, this story that waits
Has already been told,
But the words were lost as they were coming to us.

Waking, what were the names
Of the trees, the taste
Of salt licked from skin, the scent of sea blown in from a place called distance.

I am selfish, wanting this, constructing
Desire in the fold of want,
The trees, gone nameless, bend in the wind.

Asked if I had ever contemplated it, I said yes,
But knew I could never,
Since too much depended I thought on the next day.

The next day is a dream the gods have
Made their way
Across the desert, delicate and cruel, so much like ourselves.

They become us. For what else could the divine be
But the register
Of our failures, written in our own hand.

There is no single story, yours rests with
Mine, thigh to thigh,
A lamp swings above us, insects glitter briefly with what we remember.

3. Reliquaries

His limb, mine.
His water, mine.
His grove, mine.
His words and my words.
Two circles drawn, not touching.
His knife, mine.
Who will come to the altar first, with the first lamb, the first born, the first of the other
Will claim the land, the sun, the water
And wrap the other in ash and lice and burn
The claim to home and safe return
And set nothing there
As relic, the tracks leading into the hills
The only trace.
The land empty, ours.

A fossil—tooth or shell—wrapped
In cotton.
A digit, wrapped in linen, shrunken
Into amber hide.
Leaf, feather, blossom, pressed
Into the pages of a book.
Vial of sand, vial of salt, vial of water,
Sealed with wax.
Bone, maybe from femur or tibia, locked
In a hammered metal box.
Nail parings, a clutch of hair, bread, fish, the sediment

Of wine, a dried spot of semen or spit, a brick, blood on sheets,
Hypodermic, iv tubing, torn fabric, a photo of a child, a message written and lost,
The smell of honey and wet earth.

Break open the jars, the tombs.
Break open the houses, the books.
Break open the olive wood, the ground.
Break open the wounds, the lesions.
Break open the words, the seeds.
Scatter them until there is no history.
Until the faces are scrubbed out by sand.
The sand covers the roads,
And their tongue travels alone
In the beak of a crow.
This is the rule, the word,
The claim of one brother over another,
This is the story, the river that has no other
Side, no other ending, no law but this one.

Early Betrayals

Early spring rain—everything in a state of contingency:
The hawthorn is wrapped in silver gauze,

Maples' new leafing cluster like blastulas of cells,
Forsythia bracts, scales of lilac buds—

The same writing each year.
Another life takes shape among the trees—

The flies have come back, glistening clouds after each rain,
A combustion in mid-air, the world an act of recollection—

Before the black pane, everything else
Continuing, a web spun across rose canes,

Soldiers asleep at a table,
A station at off-hours, between arrivals,

How smoke hangs near the ceiling,
No one stirs; outside, grass has sent new runners across

The mulched ground dug last fall for phlox, daylilies, and hyacinths—
Who could think of arcadia now—

Or lyric, eloquence, if that is what the hawthorn's
Cloud of change proposes,

An infidelity to stillness, that perfect outline that admits nothing,
While in the distance, always at perspective's far remove,

Men come to a village and take something
And later others also bearing arms pass through:

History's passage, something taken again,
And along perspective's corridor

Every so often someone looks up then resumes plowing
Or stitching at a window, light aslant through still bare trees.

Soon enough there will be shade, the trees full,
And at the ends of long fields, darkness, earth curving out of sight,

Into its own secret, beyond habitation, the cast of light, past
Winged faces rising from fields, streets, and ruined hillsides.

Numerology

1 is tall grass,
                    many 1's together, she says, is a plain of grass;

5 is a snake, uncoiling; 7 a waterfall. The walnut tree at the end of the field,
If it were spring, would unfold ten leaves on either side

Of the whip-stem,
                        a crow in the branches, a single spot
Waiting to go—
                      numbers are signals that nothing lasts,
You can count both ways, at least, and still there is nothing finite:

Yellow-beaked grackles, hooked, back-talking in the maple,
Swipe their bills against the moss-stained trunk, then gone,
Part of the wind's calculus,

Zero is the hawk circling
Overhead, I say; no, she says it's the lake:
                                                    we all look into it, her mirror,
And find ourselves divided.

We're given a number, and that's it, he says:
We're always part of a line,
                                    then we're gone, and the line
Heals over, the fallow's groove cutting across the hillside,
The dirt wet-black from snow-melt.

Early March, galanthus bloom in the grass,
Like a clutch of small eggs—
                                    only one music now,
Pushing against stiff mud and thatch of leaves and grass,

Everything moving toward the visible,
beyond count—dog violets,
Toad lilies, foxglove, wolfbane, tickseed—

Everything an equation, additions to something already
Formed, a seed or pith we've wrapped our mouths around
As though to suck the beginning back,

To find its taste again, its one syllable,
In the air again,
above the churned black fields, the sky
silvered, shred skins of fish.

Draw straws:
she pulls the shortest, takes the wrong path, loses a leg
he pulls the middle, nothing is heard of him again
they pull the long one, their city is gone
we pull the longest, our luck, we say, but odds were with us: you are left to read this.

The numbers tell the story, he said

Chances are,
one chance in ten,
three out of five children are born
Hungry, chances disappear,
one out of three women lives below
The poverty line.

Odds are against, numbers don't lie:

Their music drifts up like day-old snow off tree limbs, long riffs,
Long as the wind,
                    coming as it does this year from the Pacific, the sad winds
                                        still carrying their isotopes off atolls,

And we pretend there's nothing there, half-lives
Split infinitesimally, tapering off like eel bones to a distant point—

The line turns faint, like shadows of children in a ring,
          dancing on a field of tailings from a copper smelting plant outside Juárez,

Coiled, copper wire is sent back north for phone lines and fasteners, tubing
For the petrochemical plants in Louisiana parishes where school texts are decades old,

Some things you have to see, he tells me.

Two stories, the same headlines:

> one in eight plant species is at risk of extinction of two-hundred and fifty tribal languages in the United States, only thirty are learned within the family: in 1968 eighty percent of Hopi spoke their ancestral language, in 1998 only thirty percent.

Two stories   of vanishing.

The numbers tell the story,
                         every minute
                                   someone is raped: now watch
The sweep of the second-hand, they say
                                   another ten hectares of forest are cut—

The numbers tell a story, draw straws, we'll see
Who makes it across the city plaza,

Who cuts off the chicken's head, who gets the morphine, who doesn't.
We'll see who plays the violin and who listens,

And who is left without sight, or fingers, or memory.
Draw straws for liver, heart, and kidney,
For rib, spine, and thigh,
For a plate of rice, a plate of fish, a plate of fruit.

---

4 the number of transformation: a window
Its outer frame missing, a pane split, no house

To hold it, the glass absorbs the light
Then throws it back into the field.

Turning to spider-scrawl in the thin wash
Of March air, everything still in exile—listen:
                                        the cherry-apple drops
Its blossoms in the muddy snow: Su Tung-p'o banished.

Walking, we find
            straw in the dirt where a hole has been filled,
A tree taken down, tire ruts, thick leaves whorl
From the thick ground—

What is ordinary joy, knowing what is to come,
Or what is here,
                crab-apple blossoms drifting across the yard
                                        or the desire to be held,

Knowing everything could turn rote,
A facsimile—and each night the fear I have accomplished that:

Tall grass, coiled snake, waterfall—
                                        I listen,
                                                  spilling: the surge and ache of wind

Cold flood, everything disappears, my only lesson.

Bee-Yards

Into stunned dormancy folded,
the bee-yards brown, no measure
for return, that rapture

Of first heat, anchorages of scents across the fields,

First flying out from clattered wings,

Veined as old leaves,
caught at this time last year in rake tines
and left hung in the dark shed,

The dormant hive, where the last ones have gathered
in winter's heart
swarm on the inmost frame

Of the super set at field's end,
everything waits for its time of setting out,
bow poised above strings, ready for the long draw-down,

In recurrence's syntax, no sentence is the last,

Or lasting, no fixity of lead or gold,

What is done in this life, swarms momentarily,
toward air, light-tossed trees.

This stretch across the north tips
Of the Finger Lakes, is a string of prisons,
From Auburn to Attica, cells orbit yards.
In Auburn, the beekeeper was the executioner,

Fastening straps and wires, the chair
Square as a box
At the center of a dark field
Where there are no windows, no paths out
To the beyond, where the eye looks
Back, nothing is let out.
This is a world where there is no forgiveness,
No reproach for the unforgiving.
Along this archipelago of lakes
Another prison opens where the clay-heavy
Ground has been turned, and earlier cross-tracks
Of bear and Seneca, land-clearings.
The beekeeper walks back from his boxes,
He is a god, overseeing his bee-races,
Hybrids of European and African honeybees
To form colonies, swarming in the bee-space between frames
That Langstroth found in 1851 optimum between combs,
Thus hives were no longer destroyed
For their honey, while union dead were buried,
And in western states, another war was undertaken,
Another land-clearing, so that thirty years later
The beekeeper could apply the new science
Of electricity to social control, understanding
That life is temporary, that
As the role of bee-killer and drone depict,
There are only the sacrificed, functionary,
And predator, and so the beekeeper built
The chair that would execute in a way that
Edison declared inhuman, but only after
He himself had demonstrated its efficacy
On cats and dogs, and his assistant Harold Brown following
In sideshows with what the press called
Electrocution experiments on hundreds of horses

And cattle. Death arrives in seconds,
Flesh cauterized,
A halo of light and smoke around
The chair, the carpenter's
Solution, an image of repose, almost comfort,
Solace to our desire that everyone should die
Without pain, while our God
Of Cruelty, the only one we can claim ours,
Made in our image, searing white,
Oversees the ministration of pain.

On the sill at winter's approach, my daughter
Picks up the dead bee, stroking its abdomen

Soft with pollen-catching hairs,
To save in a box with moth-wings and Japanese lanterns.

The queen, she tells me, lacks a stinger.
History begins with memory, the first snows

Recalled, like thin wings slipping against the glass,
Do you remember, she will say, the fox

In the stiff grass, they are always there, at the edges
Ready to carry off the parts we've forgotten,

They bury it, and come back later,
After the fields have emptied, do you remember,

She asks again. Clouds swell in the west, we lie
In the aftermath of the present, moving now

By recollection, unannullable.
In a few weeks' time the ground will be packed

By snow, one-by-one each covenant falls.
Or fails by our actions. The solitary

Bee on the sill, upturned vessel, crooked legs,
The storm's glass unscalable, the air packs

Around the words, do you remember,
Stricken by the world once we entered

That leaf-rush and convergence
Of light and wind polishing the ground,

Marking the before and after, the bee-space
The soul slides through, further.

History collapses to moments, we stitch
        bit by bit, thread and silicon wafer,
            memory's caches like amber cells stretched

Across the wafer of morning gold, like the domes of capitals,
        transmissions tethering us among the debris, horizon after horizon
            opening before us, without codes

And as though we could move without effort
        across each space, meanings held in place by another's thick gravity,
            each like a shepherd moon herding the luminous

Debris, like sentences appearing in dreams, the thread we've spooled out before
to follow back, from the underneath and lost,
our breath carrying the language of bees

If we were to return this way, swarming on the still-warm flesh, the carrion-birds
sidle off, as Aristaeus, bee-keeper and overseer,
is walking from the shadows with the last of her garlands.

Estuarine

Read
In the direction of the bird's mouth

The light almost solid, he s'd.

The word gave out, worn even
At the beginning

Each a singularity
Where collapse had reached infinity

And burst back
Read again, some new rising again

White thickening, thickets of almost color
Shadows, inexhaustible, thetic

Consider this,
Then, coming from that direction

Light a continual background
Thickening and spreading thin

In no regularity, spreading as tho'
Ships rear'd upon the horizon to be

Oar shafts
Or there, the beached rolled steel torques all rust and light

Each increment
A traveler to infinity, considered

There could be no other way

Iron Path [*Eisen-Steig*]

Consider history as a cloud or the spread of roots
Where nothing is consecutive
Except at the moment of singularity, as in when one
Walks into the day's weather,
The wind tearing the loose branches, power
Lines dipping, and perhaps this is all we could
Consider with any validity, for to go beyond this
Is to assume the passage of those whose names
We do not know, the wind sweeping through their rooms
The cracked windows overlooking the bridge
With its incessant traffic flowing away to that
Soft verdure beyond the river,
Restless with what is before us
We want to be away, is that not so,
As the edge of winter approaches, the cost
Of heat goes up, squatters light fires on the top floors
Of buildings, the whole city seems beyond
Repair in this corrosive air, light sliding
Down branches and scaffolding.
Someone calls and demands an answer,
But I am no longer in that business,
It is barely enough to recall who has died,
Or the way home,
Or the theft of what would have been.
What could we ascertain when feeling
Is fugitive, the horizon pushing its one line
Down. In this system, we are always at history's
Remove, always removed farther into
The gorse and bracken, the place of
Less and less,
Where God must have walked in despair
Collecting the trimmings and burnt
Bones, but for what

End no one of that district would
Presume, and we swerved off the road
The sudden wind
Winter's edge
The bridge, the formation
Of sounds falling
Back, each narrow
Tendon, stilling.

This occurs when the "same" extends across different fields
for example, chair and the text describing chair and an image
of that chair, does any domain then differ in our synchronic
apprehension of it all, as though there was nothing more here
than met the eye, in other words, an attempt to purify
the experience, to just that, to the point of the impossibility
of figure or necessity, but just that seen there and there.

The erasure of evidence is the demand that power makes,
for without that evidence there is no witness. History can
only be the record of erasure, thus in itself complicit with
power. It is as if, pulled from the firing squad, one said
"I am alive. No you are dead." And then after years have passed,
to write, "Later," "I remember," or "I know," as though
to assure us of the testimony, its accuracy, its place in time.

Who is that coming through the forest
—A man bearing a flaming tree.

Who is that at the far end of the room
—Someone in the shadows, we don't know.

Who has stacked the books in the libraries
—Those who have not been allowed to read them.

Whose portrait is that floating in the black ink
—It is not a portrait.

Whose door is that of the hut
—The door closed.

Who will open the door
—The door of the hut.

Who has lit the fires, planted the grain, closed the books
—Fire, grain, book.

Who is there
—There, there, there

Language can be considered moving toward its end so as to exist in a preserved state or toward its transformation that is away from stability; a dead language belongs to the archive where the sayable and the unsayable cease their opposition, where there is no estrangement, except from the living, yet among the living to be estranged corresponds the loss of the sensory, to confess one's loss.

Always the continuing erosion: the wood retreats week by week, the late winter mud expelling vestige objects—coin, worked flint, glass, ceramic—each signaling the fracture between presence and loss as they are turned over and over in our hands. Beyond us, light snow drifts down through ash, maple, birch. What language remains intact, capable, beyond the names—beyond what is sufficient is betrayal.

Of course, the perspective continues
Deeper into the field.
What is there
If we could think of it
Would be still outside
Our words, even what we know of it
Remains not in question
But a sharp pain that continues
Like the perspective line
To some end we have no idea of.
And to consider those already there,
Transported on these lines
And lost to sight:
The sky churns, and what token
Could we offer to what is ahead
But would be cast aside,
Like a torn olive branch,
A figure
Of speech, the fleeting
Light we walk in.

From a Proposed Notebook from the Country

If on taking a walk, the wind
Punctured by birds,

The path awash with
Locust petals—

The landscape is dream before
Each particular swims up into our touch

In that meadow we were moving
Slowly through the grasses

The wind an eddy pulling us
Through the harbors of plantain and mullein—

No end, no forgiveness, no eternity
Under the fireballs and reflective spheres of ice

Here the hard scrabble of rock and clay,
Dust we bathe in to come back skin

And bone; petal by petal dropped
Seed-sprung, and wind-driven.

We've invented time's calculus,
Knuckle of chalk, marrow-drained digits,

To count our way past
Each burn and lesion, each tremor

An array of possible failings, then
The weather changes.

Then, what rapture, the century counts upon
As it ends, squirrels in the attic

Raining for days, the cold drilling our bones
Despite the calendar's reckoning,

The locust tree outside the kitchen window
In a sidelong glance a stranger

Coming to the door, coming back to the house
To reclaim what was left—

The light sifted out the extraneous,
The castings left for us,

What was there leaves only that last
Reference of shed

Skin or shell, husk or plaster,
Scattering on the leaves, pond-skins of cloud and hyacinth,

The meadow-bog with its iris lifting airward,
All to break-down, and re-enter

A relentless coming-back,
Atom by atom—

And, after taking the path at the edge of pines,
Their scent almost a fog after the rain,

Resin globing on the trunks, the light itself amber,
In the night something has crashed through the weeds

Where the pines give way to maple saplings, everything
Defined by edge and boundary, the abrupt

Drop from shadow into light, consonants
Signal a margin where grass gives

To air and crow flying: imagine a place
Of no desire, the crow falls, what is known

And unknown align, the forest path gives out
And we are not lost, the locust petals

Sifting in the grass are only locust petals
And nothing more could be proposed

Or taken from or written after, no shadow crossing the window
Or vowel to curl tongues around—

And something moving in the space between, watery, ourselves
Between the body and the meadow,

Between desire and thought, if the two could be pulled
Apart, that is

The work of centuries, when all work is but writing
In a day-book, a sifting, a coming back to,

To find the pine a meadow, the rock water,
The dust made into vowel, then—

Then is artesian, rock cleft, what begins, or means to be,
And now,

What is there, opening out, calyx, hyacinth, water meadow,
The O's of fish tasting the other element,

O desire, against the rack and knuckling
Marched against us,

Steam rising then risen from fields, letting go
Before the dark rim of trees

Where ravine or river creases the landscape going dark of our words
Going dark of each particular, each awash—

At night, in the country, the skies press their lanterns,
So many boats, votives lit,

Crossing already to the other side,
Leaving the sealed envelopes, the locust

Branches, thorned and leaf-ribs
Webbing the gone light, deep

In night's groin the rush of traffic
And the other side merciless in the unraveling of souls.

Land of Two Rivers [*Zweistromland*]

Meanwhile
Systems, in effect
Modalities of delivery,
Discharge increments of the known,
Messages conveyed as packets, dosages
Of heparin, for example, released
Into the orders of the body,
From the ordinary
Erosions defining
Time's presence
The treatment
Regulated as it were
By series of dams
Earthen, sand, cement, and the landscape
Tips, there is a lake, instead,
Rivers running into it roil,
And below, the forests turn to mire,
The systems are up and running,
To the south, the cities are lit
A dome of light washing out
The low stars—
Think of it as hearts giving out,
For example,
Where capacity cannot
Match demand, depleted
Of oxygen, fluids pool and turn
To mire in the extremities, the reaches where
We are present, even touching you
If it were you this time,
And meanwhile,
Systems continue to monitor
The conditions
As rods descend into pools,

Cooling ponds silt-up,
Containment dams stretch across the bay,
Someone is out there
Walking,
The gulls are overhead,
Bright as stars—yes?—bright as stars
As it were, long ago,
Two rivers
Cradled
Sheltering fires, first
We were taught,
Then spreading,
Thus it could be said,
Always depending upon
Systems of delivery, gauging
The spread
From first impact
Of light, its rapidity, across the ground.

The Drought

for Michael Ives

A dream of water
Deluge delirium a fever—
On a hillside in a time of drought
To feel the dirt sifted
Under years of ants' milling
Hardened
As palate or bone
To turn desire-
Less, or undesired, a
Dream of water sub-
Siding deep
Into the ground below well-point
Or aquifers' marrow—
To read
Dryness
Tongue curls around the pit
Of a word, waiting
For departure
Across floods
That have not come
Bridges suspended
Over the ravine
Toward scabbed hillsides

———

The language of symptoms
Turns away
Desire—sumac and maple saplings bloodied
In the October light—
Everything then is *trespass* and

Driven from,
The light bearing its rods
Bears down upon us
Counting out our wrongs—
Parables coming to us from the other side
Of the door, *too little time, too little time,*
Have you? Those from the Watchtower
On their rounds, with gold-capped teeth,
Hum on, leaf-spines
Litter the walk.

Curled tongues of buckeye leaves
Reddened and falling in August
Striated blades of iris, the wasting
Of tissue, the susceptibility
To infestations of borers—
Pines choke, rings contract.
Hummingbird over globes of beebalm,
The dream of water
In its eye,
The dream of water turning still,
And we cross over it
Into the thing we cannot know,
Braided into another
Sequence, one point after another,
Each one a saturating
Globe slung there,
There, there.

The dwindling and absent tallied,
The history of inflictions govern tongue and organ,
Bone and fluid.
Spread on hard ground.
Spread on hollow reeds and blades.
In the torso of light
Moving under the trees
So slowly it could be you
Or, if not you, a flock
Of doves, a likeness,
Remnants,
Diving against the light
Then upwards again,
A sheen of memory,
Like a dream of water.
And as we skate across it
The tree line recedes
On the far side.
We skate farther
And farther, the arc
Of the world bowing the water
The dream of water solid and cold
We move across,
Until to someone watching
We would be lost
To sight, which predicates a subject
And an autonomy
Of movement and gaze,
And that within those lines
We could disappear, and
In fact, such autonomy

Includes that possibility, if not that fate,
That in the tally of subjects
A subtraction is at work.

And then
To almost nothing,
The soil of names
Mullein and milkwort,
Always coming back
Tight-rooted and profuse,
Always the where to begin
And then the what follows—
The ground fills with the course of things—
A car backfires,
Carpenter ants channel through wood.
Nothing stops
But spreads,
Thinning to air, water, sound.

A Matter of Wind, or [*Das Goldene Vlies*]

the surface swept
in sheer transition, all
drifted,
and you, through winter
wheat   ocher
chaff   wind
dust   straw
-drift
in the sea's
chime   across bitter grass
nails   glass

which arc
demarcated passage
east
then again
west   which star
followed as its
enormous gears
spewed teeth across
the surfaced
earth

and you
caught in the wind's
valence   its sentence
housed transit   delayed
flight across
the chimed grass   ice
-sheathed

while at the poles
of your travels,

which paradise
did you
figure   outside of transit
rested solely
separated from all cause

we could be
always nearing as
you discard
all shadow
ashen dresses   photos
loops of film
of ourselves   over
-exposed   fading
as you too
so depart across
that dark water
into that copse
that dark land

with whose name
do we call you
back from those
fields where
the dead are watched
and masked bees
arc like gold
pulled
from the heaps,
—of what, of what—
as you move on
and we call
in vocables already

remote   burning
away like straw
lead   mercury
or

swifter elements
dispersed
in wind
past sea
-oats and eucalyptus   drift
-wood   that
pearled ever
-lasting   we saw

Rifts

Physics allows that the sum
Of everything could be
                held in the smallest orb

Or that which we watch for at the other end of time
      and what is thought to be

The center
         if for only a moment

Before its sudden foliation
                    the moment we are in—

Undressed and moving towards
                    each other in half-light

As though deep
Winter lasts a fraction then

Bees carry their palanquins
Into fields whose

Ground is breaking up—

We dream in landscapes
                of convected air

Between sheets of heat and cold—

Across the lake
              the air fills

In the absence above the surface
With its own braiding of light

Gulls wheel through
                  fretted colors

Spilled from explosions of particles
Colliding—

The same could be said of desire
Finding itself always the absent space

Filling its own first scarcity

Above the flood of water and the ground's
Hold of bulbs and roots,

The milk-drop grubs wintering under ice-threaded
Dirt and snakes coiled around

The cold unheaved stone under garden leaves—

Human skin as smooth as lake water

Smooth as windows snow spirals upon

Smooth as that darkness

You move through night-blind

Air and skin one skein drawn

And drawing

Desire everywhere in before

Rift and seizure

The throttling wind

Gap and edge

Ice ledge   lip palate

The sky keening above

Always signaling in its static fallout

What is wanting

What is Wanted

Little news could be added except to note
that the steady decline had accelerated,
discussions were failing:
driving from one section
of the city to another where
the bombing had intensified,
but re-routed at the last moment,
the areas of greatest damage
went unseen, though stories
always filter back alongside
the news reports that seldom
mention casualties, nor the instructions
the army carries out in the territories
where special permits are required
prior to any movement if you are
not a citizen, or if you are a resident
but not a citizen, or if you are a
citizen but not an enfranchised citizen,
and even then it is difficult
and explanations are closely
attended to so as to receive
what is wanted, a clean slate
or good review, a report that suggests
everything remains under control,
and such incidents are unremarkable.
It is like driving to the city's
center we know has suffered,
but turned away, and like water
seeping through a roof, driven by gravity,
searches for the path of least resistance
along the rafters and joists,
through the plaster, finally
weeping through, seen at last

along a crooked seam or crack,
flaring out, feathering concertina wire,
that turns us back, to count our own
extremities while looking out
over a field, the grasses whipped
gold by the sun.

• • •

Our own bodies map out the world
that we made for ourselves.
Cratered, the city is my own
heart and I am the gun unloosed.
I am the city of Cain
where Abel was driven from,
and into my heart:
harboring Abel, I search him out
with the eyes of Cain.
The fields are laced and wired.
Birds rise up from them,
then surge down like combers, settling
into the thick grass,
only what is lightest can trespass.
What is wanted is innocence
or what remains of it, buried
in scar tissue so thick it begins
to choke arteries and the air seems
thinner, so thin our breath is pulled
from us before we can swallow.
The city glints in the steep sun,
turning a corner, there are no buildings
only their ruins, and farther,
along the hillside, the corps

is bulldozing a fruit grove,
a house in flames.
All night I will roll in my sleep
shouting for Abel.

• • •

And if he should come,
when the day's heat pressures the city,
flattening the fields
and hillside ruins,
we know what we would do this time,
we would not think this time
will be different,
we will not pause longer and ask
if he is weary from his travels,
we will not forget our jealousy,
we will not forget our desires.
And if he should come,
we know where he has kept his knives,
the whetstone, and block.
We remember how he hoisted the lamb
and drew the blood into vessels,
how he grabbed the young goat
by its first horns with his grass-stained hand
and sheared the skin off deaf to its cries and the terror
of the other animals,
while our grain was scattered
and the fruit trees sagged, ripe fruit
unwanted, and if he should come,
would he come this time for our children,
to hoist them above his block.
We were not chosen, except to be

his scapegoat, except to be the prey
of our own rage, even as our fruit
turned gold with the orbits of bees
and the welling up of nectar.

Scripting

1.

Dreams assemble all day
Fissured and wrapping
Around themselves curled
Into each other's body

Snow clouds over
The plains hundreds of miles away
Sweep across the topographies of
Gyri and sulci where
Tree
Bird
Fox form after their figures

Retreat
The blur of snowfall smearing out
The far hill carrying the trace of gulf and river valley
Ore tailings and air-hung
Residues
Half-lives arriving each night

A burst of birds surging out of the thrashed fields
In a boil of flight then subsiding—
                                                  what fires
Them and retreats
Remains unseen
Always underneath

2.

We travel through sleep—
Long-distance swimmers
Whose only rule is not to think what

Travels below
Pelagic and devouring
All night the chop and swash
Between combers

Debris and sewage drifts to push through—
The interpretation is anger
The pull of currents draws us away

From landfall
Creasing the surface
Where sediment falls away for miles
Below—
If I were to stop I would begin my drift

Downward
Losing breath
As one might lose memory and touch
Until there is nothing but descent

Into lung and bone crushing pressure
But to keep churning, the escort boat's floodlights
Dipping between crests
Deep into this

Skin no longer holding
My body's water against the sea-swells

Then hauled out
Welts from jellyfish polka-dotting

Arms and legs
Gray-blue fins
Of sharks rasping the boat
Elsewhere flares are lit for others

3.

This is one history:
Abydos to Sestos.
Landfall written as desire.

After arrival, the summing up, standard to any history
Or dissection report, the landscape
Suffused in gold and

The usual codas, strangers greeting each of us,
A recollection begun, *the leaves silvered in the wind*
By way of conclusion

To mark understanding,
That the minute is inescapable, that entity is notable,
A line drawn from eye to hand to far stone

Field, shore, breast, cock,
You could substitute what you will
Until all subsides after

That friction, the swimmer disappears, one hand
In air—yours or mine in this piece?—
But this after the ending,

Beginning another reflection, the daily work
That keeps piling up between
Each other, beginning a history of labor

Of articulation and what was said
Is obsolete if not inseminated
With that one spot, where the light comes down

On the dark ocean as a circle of gold
Someone is
Swimming in.

4.

It is its own content

Like oil in sand

Or followed into the woods

Everything turns into writing   he wrote

Last   at 5:15 a.m.   *I'll drown my book*
Before the last letter was erased

Blinds drawn and

Periodicity ended when the flesh was peeled back

But how do we account for the losses

And construe from fragments that landscape

She wanted to leave it with you

When the river broke

The dream anatomized

5.

She whispers *the large ones*
Arrive through the back those
Are the nightmares while the small ones
The good dreams come
Through the back of the left hand

6.

Each night owl-wind
No outline
Only the disturbance
Of passage
Thin snow filling in
The cavities of trees

Then release it to travel
Into shadows a fox crosses
Before it is no longer

There only the path
Worn like the dip of spine

Cuts across meadow
Out of sight a wolf or rat
Always ungoverned
                              shades
Of wolf
Rat
Weasel
In the thick hay-grass
She sees them
Thick gray
Moving into
Thin snow spinning across the meadow.

The Order of Angels [*Die Ordnung der Engel*]

What new world is this: a

Pillar of cloud poured, and look she cried

The sea, pouring beyond that line

What work is to be yet done, the stones

Uncoiled snakes, the orders ascend in air,

And look, the earth furrowed as in the tilling at late

Winter, the farmhand not seen, but perhaps

Looking up, the sky leaden, of course, she said

The cloud a stone molten and pouring upon

The land tilled before they set forth

* * *

The danger here is not the question of forgetting,
But the repression of why we remember

Ecstatic as we walk among the ruins, thinking
Of that lost splendor, that seduction

That now spent leaves us melancholy, forgetting
What it was we were not immune to,

How we succumb again to the beautiful, dreaming
Of lines of columns receding, everything at last

In its place, to be found always suffuse and glowing,
Not the straw scattered among the furrows

Catching the long slant of November, mudded and ebbing
To the far fields, no order of angels, no light

To rescue our thought, no art for solace, nothing
Is what is here but the daily, no rescue.

• • •

How do epochs end, we wondered, *scarlet as*
Phoenician sails, that soaked up the light and the air,
Lavish for a moment, lavished upon us,
Then that empty sea again, the curtain to this window
Bellying out, pregnant with wind, with what
Is coming, after the night, after the lindens
Have rustled in the night, the sea along the jetties
Stirring, the horizon where we watched the sails,
Watched for their arrival and then disappearances,
What little order there really was,
Except this, the light, the air, what was coming,
What has passed at last inaudible, its wake
A wave among waves pushing against shore.

• • •

In the painting, the stones, or rather rolled
Congealings of straw and mud, are labeled
One through nine, and arranged semicircle
At our feet, then lead lines stretch to names
Struck at the horizon, of each order,
As though this were a garden laid out

Last season, or at early spring almost
Too early for germination. Running
Counterpoint to the ruts or furrrows
Of the heath, the lines fade to the lead
Fog, and at the top of the painting, for
This is a painting, in rough script, naming
Dionysius Areopagite, witness to this
Scene, his work, or our surrogate,
As we are always coming from the forests,
To the fields, the words rustling out of
Stones and winter's grass, their first
Names, the powers of those names
Their brutal pressure as we stare at them,
At where we have come from and what
Some whisper we move toward, without
Power, insignificant, in this painting.

• • •

The snow falls heavily now
In the painting, it blurs the hills, the city.
I am in the memory of the painting,
The door to its dominion of lines,
Of the scrubbed lead at the blur of horizon.
And what if it didn't happen here,
Or this way, or at all, this field with wet
Straw, clods of stone and clay, just fields,
Just my memory of fields, that nothing
Had happened, that nothing continues
To weigh heavily, as it must.
Which kingdom would this be,
Which memories would I have,

When would it have happened?
And captive to which history, then?

• • •

Belief, otherwise, is a calamity.

• • •

And if there were: *Once I entered the chapel, and from the heat that already prevailed in the city even in the early morning of that day, and stood before the three rows of frescoes that cover the walls up to the ceiling, I was overwhelmed by the silent lament of the angels, who have kept their station above our endless calamities for nigh on seven centuries. Their lament resounded in the very silence of the chapel and their eyebrows were drawn so far together in their grief that one might have supposed them blindfolded.*

• • •

When we arrived the mosquitoes were thick upon us

Arrived from Thrace, overland, all emptied there, bloodied

The Atlantic heav'd upon us mightly, before

The ground was thick with growth, the streams ran fast with salmon and trout

When we arrived we were beset upon

When the others joined us, we raised thanks and slew

The Atlantic heav'd and so we drew together, which psalm

And among us we cast out

Among the boulders, the gravel screes

Coming from Thrace, or further, in exile in Tomis, what fields lay there,

Coming as we did, Vulci, here too, the arch with

Coming here, my name scratched on the lime

Thick as thieves, thick as fleas, they all sang

Which among us cast out first

Or from Kyzyl, Scythian burials there we watched in deep weather wrapped

Arriving paid out first come swart and fallow

Among us thick and rejoindered the Atlantic heaving

The world clay and lime, watersheds waterfowl terns the wide breadth of grasses

Land bridges and the heave of

Wrapped in the sky a blister of cold eye tearing

First palm then face that history to come, drawn likeness

Here we are, still, beyond us it goes on and on

Trundled into distances, soon to be wagon heaps and dog traces

The Atlantic there, bearing down, glacial scree traversals

There, there there

To pull ashore, toss the severed hand inland and make our claim first

Estuarine

Curvature meets
So little resistance
Reeds hollowing as though
The gods had at last come

Sweeping through the world,
The gods,
Just "they," you think,
Whittling what comes

Down to just the wind,
Or less, something settling
Across the bends, the curves
So little resistance

To each shift of light and wind,
As though the gods were keeping
The light from
Failing, falling from

That blue, and somewhere,
Yes, they launched
Upon the curvature
A call towards,

Whom, it is said the votives lit
Coming in light, yellows upon
White, thinned to this,
Pronoun, utterance

To keep that outside, that secret
Outside, that name, beyond

What resistance or pressure
Of knowing, named, beyond

Trespass or bend of
Trajectory, yellow to white
Dripping in the fogged light,
They calling, they there

White among shimmer
Reeds hollow,
Convergences among
Script and light

Notes

"Estuarine": all three poems titled "Estuarine" refer to Cy Twombly's series of paintings *Coronation of Sesostris* (2000).

"The Sand Runs Through [. . . *Es Rinnt Uns der Sand aus den Haaren*]": title from Anselm Kiefer's painting of 1997.

"Birth of the Sun [*Geburt der Sonne*]": Cited passages from Alain Badiou's *Ethics: An Essay on the Understanding of Evil.* Title from Anselm Kiefer's photographic sequence of 1987.

"The Burning of the Rural Districts [*Ausbrennen des Landkreises Buchen*]": title from Anselm Kiefer's bound photographic volumes of 1974.

"Star-Gown [*Sterntaler*]": Egyptian funerary objects of Merytamun and Tutankhamun in the Metropolitan Museum of Art; quote in section two from Giacomo Leopardi's *Zibadone.* Title from Anselm Kiefer's painting of 1991.

"Reading Bashō to My Daughter": prose from Nobuyuki Yuasa's translation of Bashō's *The Narrow Road to the Deep North and Other Travel Sketches.*

"Canaan": Methods of torture used by Israel's General Security Service as reported by Amnesty International: *shabeh:* where a prisoner's hands and legs are tied to a chair in an uncomfortable position; *gambaz:* squatting for long periods of time; *tiltul:* violent shaking, which may cause brain damage.

"Iron Path [*Eisen-Steig*]": section 2 refers to Joseph Kosuth's *One and Three Chairs* (1965); the quotes in section 3 are from Maurice Blanchot's *The Instance of My Death;* section 4 references Anselm Kiefer's painting *Mann im Wald* (1971); section 5 is adapted from Giorgio Agamben's *Remnants of Auschwitz: The Witness and the Archive.* Title from Anselm Kiefer's painting of 1986.

"A Matter of Wind [*Das Goldene Vlies*]": in reference to Anselm Kiefer's painting of 1990.

"Land of Two Rivers [*Zweistromland*]": title from Anselm Kiefer's photographic sequence of 1989.

"Scripting": section 4: lines in italics from Ted Berrigan's *The Sonnets.*

"The Order of Angels [*Die Ordnung der Engel*]": section III: passage in italics from Adam Zagajewski's "Sail," from his collection *Canvas;* section VII: passage in italics from W. G. Sebald's *Vertigo;* section VIII: Thrace, from Ovid's *Metamorphosis,* XIII; Vulci, Etruscan site; Tomis, Ovid's exile. Title from Anselm Kiefer's painting of 1983–4.

JAMES McCORKLE lives in Geneva, New York, with his wife and two young daughters. He received the M.F.A. and Ph.D. from the University of Iowa, as well as fellowships from the Ingram Merrill Foundation and the National Endowment for the Arts. He is the editor of *Conversant Essays: Contemporary Poets on Poetry,* and the author of *The Still Performance,* a study of postmodern poetry.